HINTS

SUSAN T. RAY

PUBLISHED BY WESTVIEW, INC., NASHVILLE, TENNESSEE

PUBLISHED BY WESTVIEW, INC.
P.O. Box 210183
Nashville, Tennessee 37221
www.publishedbywestview.com

© 2009 Susan T. Ray
All rights reserved,
including the right to reproduction
in whole or in part in any form.

ISBN 978-1-935271-14-7 hardcover
ISGN 978-1-935271-15-4 paperback

First edition, July 2009

Printed in the United States of America on acid free paper.

For

My Mama and Daddy

Don and Elizabeth

Christy and Robert

"No man was ever so completely skilled in the conduct of life, as not to receive new information from age and experience."

Terence (190-150B.C.)

Introduction

The idea for this book grew out of an interview I heard with Captain Chesley "Sully" Sullenberger. He was the pilot of a US Air Ways jet that suffered a bird strike to both engines and ended up in New York's Hudson River, January 15, 2009. In the interview, the Captain stated his belief that everything he had done in his life, up to the moment of the US Air incident, prepared him for the actions that he took that day, resulting in his landing that plane without a single loss of life. His experience as a combat pilot, licensed glider pilot, accident investigator and commercial airline pilot all combined to give him the depth of knowledge to face such an incredible challenge that could have resulted in great tragedy but instead, ended in triumph.

~ Hints ~

I thought about Captain "Sully's" interview in the light of my own life and wondered if I were ready for a 'Hudson River' experience of my own.

I was fortunate to have been raised in a loving family, with a spiritual foundation and, because of that, I have always believed in 'the life to come.' Due to that belief, in large part, I began to think of all the ways God has given me many, many 'hints' about that life. I believe that others have experienced similar 'hints' too but may not have recognized them as such. Thus this book came to be.

It is my hope that anyone who reads this work will come away with at least one smile, one ah-ha moment, one insight and a reason to rejoice in one more day.

There is one other reason why I wanted to put some of my thoughts down on paper. In my lifetime, I have heard some individuals attribute many horrible motives to God. Some have presented their Creator as hateful, petty, insensitive to and detached from His creation. It is my belief that such attributions could not possibly be further from the truth. If nothing else, I hope at least one reader comes away from this book really liking God.

Contents

1. May I Help You? 1
2. Yeast Rolls 5
3. Museums 9
4. Daddy 13
5. All Work is Honorable 17
6. Showtime 21
7. Clover Chains 25
8. Chicken and Dumplin's ... 29
9. Dedication 33
10. Bumbler 37
11. Puzzles 41
12. Heaven's Gain 45
13. Look Around 49
14. Gone Fishin' 53

15. Full Circle 57
16. Under Construction 61
17. Treasure Islands 65
18. Beeeeep, Beeeeep, Beeeeep 69
19. Who? 73
20. Surprise 77
21. Learning Curve 81
22. Produce Department 85
23. Canes, Walkers and Wheelchairs ... 89
24. Thank You 93
25. Healing Hands 97
26. Dreams and Reality 101
27. Why Evil? 105
28. Once Upon a Time 109
29. It's a Wrap 113
30. To Teach 117
31. Lace 121
32. Little Ones 125
33. Our Big Brother 129
34. Fidelity 133
35. WOW! 137
36. Eyeglasses 141
37. Pews 145
38. The Best Pancakes in the World .. 149

39. Electronics	153
40. Gone But Never Forgotten	157
41. Recipes	161
42. Motives	165
43. Dresses	169
44. Anticipation	173
45. Be Still	177
46. Doughnuts	181
47. An Apple and An Orange	185
48. Sleigh Ride	189
49. The Kitchen Window	193
50. Old Broadway	197
51. Christmas Eve	201
52. Hide and Seek	205

~ 1 ~

"Life is the childhood
of our immortality."

Johann Wolfgang von Goethe (1749-1832)

May I Help You?

I imagine, at one time or another, everyone wonders what they are doing here. I know I certainly have.

When I was much younger, I really believed that I would change the world, do something really noteworthy, and accomplish BIG and significant things. Those ideas may well reflect the universal prospective of the young. But, for me, none of those things happened.

At one point, in my working life, I believed I would become well-known for brilliantly executing my craft. Needless to say, that did not happen either. True, I loved what I was doing but was not destined for fame and fortune by any stretch of the imagination.

As the years passed, I did ask myself: "What are you doing here?"

I have tried to recall just when it was that I truly made a difference. Thinking about such things is a huge 'hint' about the life to come.

I do believe that the best thing I ever did was care for my Mama during her last months with us. That was the privilege of my life.

How about a thick-sliced BALONEY sandwich? (Not BOLOGNA, as the purist would say but just good, ole, Southern BALONEY!)

When my brother was in the hospital, he had little or no appetite. One day though, he said he really would like a thick slice of baloney, on white bread, with mayo. The dietary department said that they did not have it. So, I went down to dietary and found the supervisor. I explained to her that my brother really wanted a sandwich. She had the chef cut the baloney, extra thick, and she got the bread and the mayo. With that, I carried the 'feast' up to my brother's room. He said: "That is the best sandwich I have ever eaten!" Only a few days after that, my brother took a turn for the worst and left us for his new life.

~ Hints ~

In the life to come, I will ask God why I was here. God will reply: "To take care of your Mama and get your brother a baloney sandwich." Now, that is BIG.

Why are you here?

Spend some time this week mulling it over, as I did. You will get a 'hint' of your life to come. The answers you come up with will be BIG, Important, and Life Changing for you and for those you love. God will smile the entire time you are mulling and that's no baloney!

~ 2 ~

"Give us this day our daily bread."

Matthew 6:11 NAB

Handle With Care

My Mama made the best yeast rolls one can imagine. They would melt in your mouth! Oh, the aroma of her fresh baked bread–yum, yum!

Mama never could use "that old, dry yeast," as she put it. We had to go out and find the little cakes of fresh yeast for her.

I watched her bread making with fascination but I never wrote down the process, so I can not perform her magic. I do not think I could duplicate it anyhow since I am convinced it would take my Mama's love to make her bread.

She told me, over and over, that the trick was never to handle the dough too much. She said that doing so would make the bread tough.

I can still see her with flour on her hands and sometimes on her nose, as she wove her baking spell. Those little hands had the perfect touch and produced dinner rolls, loaf bread and awesome cinnamon rolls. She'd use a jelly jar to cut out the rolls and they were a meal in themselves.

Real butter–she only wanted real butter for her bread. My Mama was an advocate of all things REAL.

Watching the care my Mama took when making bread was a real 'hint' of the life to come.

God does not pound and knead us into submission; He is gentle in His dealings with us. He is always easing us in His direction and lets our 'rising' take as long as it takes. I have always felt God knows just how to bring me to my ultimate happiness, just like my Mama knew how the dough felt in her hands and when everything was just right for a perfect outcome.

~ Hints ~

Do you know anyone who is an artist in the kitchen? Have you ever passed a bakery, at just the right time, and smelled the baking bread? You are getting 'hints' all the time. Do not miss them.

In the life to come, you will find out how God has cared for you with infinite gentleness, easing you along. Sometime, you responded and at other times, you resisted.

This week, make a conscious effort to respond in the most complete way that you can when you sense a gentle prompting from God.

~ 3 ~

"Very sacred is the vocation
of the artist..."

John of Haddington (Brown) (1722-1787)

Museums

Art museums have always been one of my favorite places to visit. I am fascinated by what artists can produce. It amazes me every time I view a wonderful painting.

Once, when I was in Spain, I went to an art museum. As I was slowly working my way through each room, I passed through a doorway and just glanced to my left. I literally jumped. Hanging on the wall, right at my eye level, was a portrait of a soldier; just his head and shoulders. It was so real that I thought someone was actually peeping at me through the wall. I have no idea just how long I studied that painting. How did the artist do it? This is just a painting on canvas. Why does it look so 3D? I was mesmerized.

~ SUSAN T. RAY ~

I remember seeing a floor to ceiling painting once, in a New York museum. It was the most spectacular work I had ever seen. Even now, if I close my eyes, I can see that painting.

What great art work always does for me is offer 'hints' of the life to come.

I guess most people may think their lives 'are what they are.' I have come to think of my life as similar to those great art works I have seen. I assume that everything is very dimensional, right now, but in reality, I am like paint on a flat canvas compared to what will be revealed in the life to come. God will show me and all of us, fullness of life in His presence.

Artists help us so much by using their talents to reveal a view of life we may not have considered before. How do you look at art? Think about it. What does any kind of art have to say to you?

Sometime this week, if you see something lovely, made by man, pause and take a moment to give it some thought. It is a 'hint.' In the life to come, God will show you the absolute truth and beauty inherent in all art because He is the preeminent Artist. You are His greatest work of art. Isn't that wonderful?!

~ 4 ~

"Children have more need of models than critics."

Joseph Joubert (1754-1824)

Daddy

My Daddy was a well-known personality in our town. He was a big man (6'7"); strong and wise. He was also a very self-possessed person; quiet and gentle in his demeanor.

When I was little, I thought my Daddy was the greatest man in the world. (That opinion has not changed over time.) He made me feel safe. He was always the wonderful protector of my Mama and our family.

I clearly remember calling anything I saw, that was large, "Daddy-sized." Daddy and Mama had a specially made bed, years before the idea of king-size beds was thought of and I called it "Daddy-size." There was a whole list of "Daddy-sized" items: Giant Hershey bars; Daddy's shoes (size 15); Daddy's lounge chair and hassock; over-sized, round dining table...

Even as a child, God was giving me a 'hint' of the life to come. Being my Daddy's little girl brought even greater meaning to the words: Our Father.

God must be something like my Daddy. I believe He is strong, wise and gentle because He gave me those 'hints' in my Daddy. I can be safe with God in my life; my loved ones can be safe; all humanity can be safe.

In the life to come, I will forever be that little girl, secure with my "heavenly Daddy."

Have you ever had someone in your life like I did with my Daddy? Did you ever think of God giving you a 'hint' of the life to come by placing that person in your life?

At some point this week, just think about the possible 'hint' you may have been given by that person. Think of the characteristics you see in that individual. Imagine all of those qualities raised to the level of perfection, in God, and appreciate your 'hint' of the life to come.

~ 5 ~

"Without hearts there is no home."

Byron George Noel (1788-1824)

All Work Is Honorable

I was really fortunate, when I started trying to find a job doing something I loved. It took several years of struggle but turned out well in the end. Thanks to marvelous, self-confident executives, I got the opportunity of a lifetime, working at one of the premier television production facilities in the country. I had watched the construction of that complex over several years and longed to work there and, sure enough, my dream became a reality. Upon being hired, my supervisor gave me a set of keys with the number 1 on them. Imagine that!

When I came to work on the first day and walked into such a beautiful environment, it was one of the happiest days of my life. For close to thirty years, I was fortunate to be able to tell everyone that going to work was like going 'home' and when work was over, I went home. Not everyone can say that about their job but working with so many gifted people made me just that comfortable and happy.

God gave me a 'hint' of the life to come in my work experience. The happiness I felt, each and everyday, was real and genuine. I thought this situation would last forever but it didn't. My 'hint' of the life to come is the knowledge that real happiness and fulfillment will go on forever and will never be lost again.

Sometime this week, think about a time when you felt real pleasure in your work. Think about the people with whom you share your hours of labor. Try and recall what the sentiment, 'a job well done', really means to

~ HINTS ~

you. God is giving you a 'hint' of the life to come through your work and your interaction with your fellow workers. The life to come will embody the words: "Well done, good and faithful one."

~ 6 ~

"The Lord God will wipe away the tears from all faces…"

Isaiah 25:8 NAB

Showtime

I just have to disagree with all those who say that in the life to come all tears will be wiped away.

Have you ever had something happen that made you laugh until you cried?

I worked at a marvelous television production facility for many years. Once, while we were doing a live variety show, an artist (who shall remain nameless), was singing a song from the Broadway show in which he was staring, about the life of Will Rogers. During the performance, he was to twirl a rope. In the process, the rope eased across the singer's head, ripping off his toupee, sending it sliding across the studio floor like a dead squirrel. Our very professional cameraman, reacting to the situation, followed the toupee on its 'journey.' The artist ran after his hair, slapped it back on his head, leaving the sideburn resting next to his right eyebrow. Needless to say, everyone in the place could not stop laughing. The entire crew was overcome with laughter and could hardly breathe. There were tears rolling down our faces. Of course, we simply had to go to a commercial break to allow all of us some time to recover enough to concentrate on our work.

God gave me a 'hint' of the life to come through laughter. When we are reunited with our loved ones and friends, there will be so many stories to share about this life and many of them will be very funny. It will be like the storytelling that goes on at family reunions, when family members tell tales from their youth and all the others laugh at the recollection.

The tears that come from laughter are cleansing and joyful.

~ Hints ~

Sometime this week, think about a 'hint' of the life to come you received through good humor. Think about how your ribcage ached from laughing and savor the memory. Try and recall those who shared the laughter with you and realize that your life to come will have many more such moments, for all eternity.

There will be certain kinds of tears in the life to come; tears of joy, with family and friends, amid peels of laughter.

~ 7 ~

"An uncommon degree of imagination constitutes poetical genius."

Dugold Stewart (1753-1828)

Clover Chains

When I was young, my brother, sister and I had so much fun playing in our front yard. Once, my Daddy got a large freezer and the delivery folks left the box behind. It was big enough for me to climb into and use as a playroom. We all played with that box until the rain turned it into mush and we had to throw it away.

In the spring, my sister and I could hardly wait for the grass to start growing because, along with the grass, the clover also bloomed, all over the yard. We made the most wonderful clover chains.

My Mama was the champion of 4-leaf clover finders! She rarely looked down that she didn't stand up holding a 4-leaf clover.

They seemed to appear everywhere she walked or at least we thought so since we could rarely find one.

In the fall, we made leaf houses. Daddy would rake the leaves into piles and we would take them, by the hands full, and lay out a 'house' on the lawn. We made leaf lines for walls, left spaces for door and used lines of leaves to create rooms and hallways. Then, we would sit on the ground, in the different rooms, playing house. After we had played long enough, Daddy would rake all the leaves into a huge pile and we would jump into it. What fun!

I received so many 'hints' of the life to come from using my imagination. As I think back on so many childhood memories, I see that God was there all the time, providing the leaves and clover and even letting a box be left behind for our enjoyment.

If our childlike imagination could form a 'house' from leaves or a box and jewelry from clover, just think about what an Infinite Imagination can come up with. We already have some idea when we see the heavenly bodies in the sky and all the wonders in

~ Hints ~

nature. So, I know that in the life to come, we will play, forever, in God's front yard.

When did you last let your imagination take you to a very creative place? Oh, it may only be imagination but when you use it, you receive all kind of 'hints.' Anything you can think up is just a small taste of the wonders that await you in the life to come.

Sometime this week, take the time to appreciate your own imagination. God is helping you open your mind to 'possibilities.' We all need to believe that anything is possible. In the life to come we will learn, first hand, that it is.

~ 8 ~

"…cookery…its object can conceivably
be no other than to increase
the happiness of mankind."

Joseph Conrad (1857-1924)

Chicken and Dumplin's

My brother-in-law is a giant of a man. He is a complex person and yet, he has simple tastes. It is strange that I chose the word 'tastes' because, for my brother-in-law, food holds great significance. He just loves to cook... no cookbooks, just his own creativity. This may well be due to his upbringing and the fact that his family did not have very many 'things' but, with food on the table, one was rich indeed.

My brother was gravely ill, prior to his moving on to his new life. While he was sick, he did manage to regain a modicum of strength. He happened to mention one day that he sure would like something really good to eat; something with some flavor! Well, that was all that my brother-in-law needed to hear.

My brother came over to my sister's house to spend the day and my brother-in-law started weaving his magic in the kitchen. He began boiling chicken, the water perfectly seasoned. Oh, the aroma was marvelous. Then, he started making dumplin's, from scratch. He spent ever so long mixing up the dough and rolling it out and cutting it into precise strips. My brother sat there watching with amazement.

With the chicken pulled off the bone, the broth done to a turn and the dumplin's having been added, the mixture gently simmered until we could hardly wait another moment to eat.

My brother said that he had never tasted anything any better and could not remember having seen anyone put so much time and effort into anything, particularly cooking, the way my brother-in-law had done.

God gives our family 'hints' of the life to come through my brother-in-law's enjoyment of cooking. I know that God is using all time and care, preparing for our welcome to our eternal home. The experience will be the best we have ever had.

~ Hints ~

Sometime this week, think about a fine meal you have shared with family and friends. Close your eyes and try to recall the aromas, the preparation, the presentation and the taste. Realize that you have been given a 'hint' of the life to come. God has spent all eternity planning for your happiness with Him and an outstanding meal is but a tiny 'hint' for all of us of the life to come.

~ 9 ~

"I have kept the faith."

II Timothy 4:7 NAB

Dedication

    I have always admired people who are dedicated to something. I wanted to be that kind of person too. I've tried; sometimes with more success than at other times.

    In my life, I have met some dedicated people. There is a retirement home up the street from where I live. I go there often. It is a place for retired religious Sisters. There I find encouragement and inspiration and feel at peace. There is a sense of calm around individuals who have dedicated themselves to a worthy cause.

    I work with some dedicated Doctors and Nurses. Now, like everything else in life, all are not dedicated. For some, what they do is a job. They may well be really good at their job but that is not necessarily the same as dedication. One can spot the individuals who possess an absolute commitment; individuals who have a 'calling.'

I have learned so much about the life to come from being around dedicated people. I think they get their dedication and commitment due to an instigating 'hint' from God. He is absolutely dedicated and committed and, I believe, He puts a spark of those attributes in us. Some fan that spark and the results are obvious; others let it die. For those who just cannot feed the flame, heartbreak, struggle, perhaps life itself, could be an underlying cause. But, I am convinced, that in the life to come, our God is so committed and dedicated to our good that He will care for all those with extinguished flames in a very, very tender and loving way, while rejoicing with the truly dedicated among us.

~ Hints ~

Have you ever been around a dedicated person for any length of time? Could you feel a certain air of self-possession on their part? Did you feel calm in their presence and yet challenged to live up to a higher standard? All of your feelings are 'hints' from God. You are being call to be all that you can possibly be. God wants you to thrive, here and now, and ultimately came to full personhood with Him in the life to come. Sometime this week, think about all the dedicated folks you know and draw from their good example to live a more fulfilled life yourself. If you are a dedicated person, mentor those around you to help them fan their own spark into a bright, intense fire.

~ 10 ~

"After crosses and losses
men grow humbler and wiser."

Benjamin Franklin (1706-1790)

Bumbler

The best friend I ever had was a bit absent-minded and once, he even lost his car in a very, very small parking lot.

This man was a war veteran; his plane shot out from under him in World War II. He survived to return home and become a religious minister, teacher and pastor. Plagued by some physical difficulties due to his experiences, he forged ahead toward a vocation and spirituality that proved to be incredibly edifying to those of us who knew him.

This good man possessed an outrageous sense of humor and I can still hear his resonant chuckle to this day.

My friend was oft times disorganized, disheveled, rarely on time for anything and completely self-effacing about it all.

At this point I must state, the gentleman of whom I speak was one of the wisest people I have ever known. He knew things. His upbringing, education, life experience and prayer life contributed to his being a perceptive, gentle and inspiring counselor.

God gave me a 'hint' of the life to come in the life of my friend. God was bringing home the point that I must never judge by first impressions. Those who believe that first impressions are the most lasting are incredibly short-sighted. In the life to come, there will be complete understanding and not a single snap judgment of any kind.

Sometime this week, think about the seeming oaf you have overlooked. Think about the one who may not be physically

~ HINTS ~

attractive whom you tend to avoid. You may be missing one of the greatest 'hints' of the life to come. You may be avoiding a person of remarkable intellect; someone of uncommon wisdom; an individual with the kind of humor that tickles you to your toes and a precious link between you and your Creator.

~ 11 ~

"It is not every calamity
that is a curse..."

James Sharp (1618-1679)

Puzzles

I really enjoy working on jig-saw puzzles; the more pieces the better. I like the kind with many, many hues, complex patterns, landscapes, beautiful use of light and shadow.

Once, I was putting together a 1000 piece puzzle. It depicted a waterfall, deep in the woods, bordered on either side by rough, rocky cliffs. After days and days of assembly, I came to the end and found that I lacked one piece. I was astounded; there was a piece missing. How could that be?

God gave me a 'hint' of the life to come from the missing piece of a jig-saw puzzle. I am a puzzle. All the persons, events, circumstances, joys and sorrows of my life make up the pieces, hues, lights, shadows and complexity of my puzzle. The events that did not come to perfect conclusions, the affection that was not perfectly reciprocated, the projects that just did not come to a satisfactory conclusion; all these life experiences reflect the missing piece; the coming up, just short, of my desired result. Why has this happened?

In the life to come, God will hand all of us the missing piece of our life's puzzle. In His loving plan, He wants us to realize we will never be complete until we reach our completion in the life to come.

Sometime this week, think about your own life's puzzle. Remember anyone who disappointed you in a relationship; any project you worked on that ended just a little bit less perfect than you had imagined it would; a much anticipated trip that did not go all that well. God is giving you 'hints' of your

~ Hints ~

life to come. He is gradually moving you to the realization that your total and complete happiness, your beautifully composed life puzzle, will receive its final piece from His hand, in the life to come.

~ 12 ~

"No man is hurt but by himself."

Diogenes (412-323 B.C.)

Heaven's Gain

My niece was a very lovely and an amazingly funny individual. Oh, how she could make us all laugh!

From the time she began to talk, she would constantly say, of many situations: "That's not fair!" She just could never reconcile herself to unfair treatment, outcomes or events of any kind. She was never at peace if something was not fair.

Because of the myriad of difficulties and inequities in this world, my niece struggled with life itself. I would tell her, over and over, year after year, to take a black marker and draw a line through 'fair' in all the dictionaries she came across. Still, she followed a destructive path, searching for a love, truth, kindness and fairness with no strings attached. In the end, she never did any harm to anyone or anything other than herself. Because she suffered so much, those of us who loved her suffered with her.

I got a 'hint' of the life to come from my niece. I know that all her longings and desires and dreams found their fulfillment in the life to come. That gives me hope in the midst of my own disappointments, heartbreaks and struggles; when things are just 'not fair.' I feel that, with God, my niece is smiling and saying to all of us: "I knew that life could be fair. I knew it! See everybody, God makes everything alright and I'm alright now that I am with Him."

Sometime this week, think about someone you may have lost, for whatever reason. If there was an illness or an accident or just the passage of time, God is giving you a 'hint.' In

~ HINTS ~

the life to come, your loved one is not sick, hurt, old or lacking any good quality of existence. God has filled each and everyone who is with Him to the full; they want for nothing in the life to come.

~ 13 ~

"Light is the symbol of truth."

James Russell Lowell (1819-1891)

Look Around

There is a lighting effect one can see on variety shows, from time to time. A cluster of lights is placed on the studio floor, near a cloth backdrop, in a fan-like configuration. They can be any color or ever multicolored. When illuminated, they glow from a tight center and splay outward, in a fan like display, reaching to the ceiling. I occasionally used this effect when I lit television shows. The point was simply to create a lovely environment for a performer to work within.

Well, one day, as I left work around dusk, I looked toward the west and found myself awestruck. I pulled to the side of the road and just sat in my car, transfixed. The sun had just slipped below the horizon; the sky was the palest of blue and shooting up from the spot where the sun had disappeared were wide streaks of peach colored light, fanning out into space.

I got a 'hint' of the life to come from looking around me. In my attempts at creativity, I saw, quite clearly, my amateur status in trying to be creative about anything. I could almost hear God humming a song from a Broadway show: "Anything you can do, I can do better."

The scene I observed in the evening sky thrilled me. In the life to come we will see just how God can bring every good thought, idea, work and deed to perfection.

Sometime this week, look around you. What do you perceive? Is there a particularly lovely flower out there? Is there a tiny, new, cotton-tailed bunny hopping around? Wow, look at that rainbow! Is that a red-tailed

~ Hints ~

hawk circling over head? Is there a shy violet nestled at your feet?

God is giving you 'hints' from all that you see. Each and every created thing is only a tiny sample of the glory of perfected creation that awaits you in your life to come.

~ 14 ~

"Patience is the art of hoping."

Luc de Clapiers Vauvenarques (1715-1747)

Gone Fishin'

My Daddy really loved fishing. He was not a tournament fisherman. No. When he went fishing, we had the most wonderful fish fries to look forward to. I am telling you, Daddy's catches and my Mama's hush puppies and cole slaw equaled a feast fit for a king (and a queen and all the little royals, like us).

Every year, I would watch my Daddy prepare for fishing season. He was absolutely meticulous about his reels. He would put fresh line on them and tiny drops of oil to make them spin like silk. Watching his big hands tie teeny-tiny knots in the line was very intriguing.

When it came time to plan a fishing trip, Daddy was on the phone, calling friends and preparing for an early morning departure to his favorite fishing spots. Usually there were two guys to a boat, everyone meeting at our house.

Daddy would load the boat, complete with Mama's homemade egg salad, in a big Mason jar, and a loaf of bread, all tucked away into the cooler. Then, they would be off.

Upon everyone's return home after a full day of fishing, we would run from the house and Mama would always say: "'have any luck?" Sometimes, Daddy held up a stringer loaded with fish (always displaying at least one catfish for Mama. She really loved catfish and Daddy always brought one home just for her). At other times, Daddy would just shake his head and say: "They just weren't biting today." Imagine, fishing all day, with no results.

I got so many 'hints' of the life to come from my Daddy's fishing trips. Patience, patience is the key. We must be patient in this life, as we work to accomplish our goals. In a very particular way, we must be patient with ourselves during this journey. I have never been very patient with myself but, I still believe my Daddy is teaching me the lesson in patience by my memories of his fishing trips.

~ Hints ~

Are you in a hurry? Are you always rushing from one thing to the next? Are you simply inpatient with yourself?

Sometime this week, think about a time in your life when you saw examples of calm, patient behavior. Draw on your memories of those who waited for something with real self-possession, not fidgeting or being irritable but simply being patient. Those kinds of memories are a marvelous 'hint.' Our God is infinitely patient with us and really wants us to be patient with ourselves. He knows that we are still learning and He will give us time because His patience is unending. In the life to come, we will fully realize how patient He always was with us.

~ 15 ~

"To everything there is a season."

O.T. Ecclesiastes 3:1 NAB

Full Circle

I really enjoy living in a part of the country with changing seasons (perhaps, in the middle of winter, the word 'enjoy' isn't exactly accurate).

Winter around these parts can be remarkably dull and grey. Sometimes, it's rather like being part of an old, black and white movie. We used to get a great deal more snow than we do now and, not unlike my Mama, snow has always fascinated me. So, as a rule, winters are drab but, thankfully, our winters do not last all that long.

Ever so slyly, tiny shoots start to peep out of the ground; the tips of trees begin to change, fatten up and prepare to explode with new, fresh foliage. Then, seemingly overnight, shocks of yellow appear in nearly every yard; the ole 'breath of spring'. As one drives around, looking into the distance, it appears that someone has tossed hands full of confetti into the air and it has frozen there; the dogwoods. Everyone is mulching and fertilizing and fixing flower beds that will eventually yield every color of the rainbow.

In the heat of summer, the green trees remain but many of the colored blossoms disappear. The flowers of summer had better be hardy to hang around here.

Fall reveals such an array of colors from the trees that it can take your breath away. Just standing and looking in every direction gives one the feeling of standing in the middle of a large bowl of mums.

Oh my, it's time for a light jacket... layers...heavy coats...winter is here again.

This wonderful cycle is a 'hint' of the life to come. I am not speaking of the cycle of life and death; no, I am only talking about the beauty inherent in watching the changes that occur all around us. Appreciating the wonder that change can reveal about our life, our circumstances and all those things that lie beneath the surface, is what captures my

~ HINTS ~

attention during the change of the seasons around here.

In the life to come, our drab days, blooming realizations, sun-drenched relationships and all the colors and textures of our life will reach perfect fulfillment.

Sometime this week, think about how things change all around you, all the time. For some, this can be very upsetting; some do not like change. Still, try and see change as a 'hint' of your potential, your true beauty preparing to bloom, hidden talents revealed. You are not like any other and God wants you to realize how marvelous you are. In the life to come, He will show you just how much you grew with every change and with every season in your life. As the cycles occurred, over and over, you learned, you matured and you bloomed in an extraordinary and unique way.

~ 16 ~

"...whether they work
with marble or sod,
the builder is hand and hand with God."

William H. Dunbar (1862-1949?)

Under Construction

I really like watching something being built. Once, I stood, oh, I don't know for how long, at my front window, watching robins weave their nest, high up in the bough of a Bradford pear. Amazing. Those birds actually wove twigs in a tight, circular pattern until they'd made a cozy nest.

When I was out in my yard one spring, I discovered a mound of grass clippings, near the corner of the house. All of the sudden, a tiny bunny hopped out. Upon closer inspection, I noticed that the mound of grass was lined with fur. Amazing.

I have Purple Martin bird houses in my back yard. I have to clean them before spring or the birds will not return, the way they always do, if the house is dirty. Amazing.

These birds build their nests from twigs, in a sort of grid pattern and hold it all together with mud. When the birds end up flying south for the winter, I literally have to dig out the dried mud from the floor of the house in order to get it clean. Amazing.

For months, as I drove to and from work, I watched the construction of an apartment building, from sub-basement to completion. I liked the framework, in particular, and thought that apartment would be a safe place to live.

God has given me many 'hints' of the life to come by my watching things being built. Each and every one of us is building something. A kind word, spare change in a little red kettle, a Band-Aid on a sore finger, a bag of used clothes; all of these things are our twigs, our foundation, our fur lining. We are all builders and, in the life to come, God will show us just what we have constructed. Amazing.

~ Hints ~

Sometime this week, think about something you have seen under construction (even if it were only blocks, stacked up by a child). How do you feel about the building process? God is giving you 'hints' of the life to come because, you see, each and every one of us is a work in progress and our completion will take place in the life to come. God will show us the results of our life's work; we will clearly see how all the things we did and said throughout our lifetime added up to the completed project in ourselves. Amazing. Some will be like beautiful, cozy, rough-hewn, log homes; others, like Gothic Cathedrals, with spires reaching to the sky; some, like Tudor mansions, with lovely gables and sparkling, channel-leaded, beveled-glass windows. Each and every lifelong project will be a joy to behold. Not any one will be the same as any other; all different; all unique; all precious in the sight of God.

What are you building?

~ 17 ~

"Gems…
look like fragments of heaven…"

George Eliot (1819-1880)

Treasure Islands

 I have never liked garage sales. The old saying: One man's junk is another man's treasury, never held any fascination for me. My sister-in-law, on the other hand, just loves 'em. She might even be considered a fanatic when it comes to garage sales. I do believe she has spent most of her life shopping at and giving gifts from garage sales.
 I believe my aversion to such pursuits came from my Mama. She was not an advocate of shopping, period. It was too time consuming. Mama would simply call the store, see if it had the item she was looking for, have them put her name on it and drop by later and pick it up.

I really got a 'hint' of the life to come from thinking about garage sales. The more I contemplate the whole experience, the more I become convinced that God likes the idea. As a matter of fact, He may be the best garage sale shopper of all time.

In the life to come, God will show us all the 'treasures' He has gathered from earth's garage sale. We will meet the homeless man who loved God but struggled with life; the prisoner who never had one single visitor during the entire time he was incarcerated; the veteran who suffered with PTSD; the teen Mom who had nowhere to go; the baby who starved to death because the dictator of the child's country wanted to have a feast. We will see how the overlooked in this world shine like precious jewels in the life to come.

I am looking at garage sales and those who like them in an entirely different light.

~ HINTS ~

Sometime this week, pause when you see someone you might have previously looked away from. Ask yourself if that someone might have been handpicked by God as His special treasure from mankind's garage sale.

As you think about all this, perhaps you yourself feel like a garage sale item or just someone's junk. God is giving you a 'hint' of the life to come. You may have spotted a future heavenly gem or perhaps, the future celestial jewel is you.

~ 18 ~

"Conscience warns us as a friend
before it punishes as a judge."

Leszinski Stanislaus (1677-1766)

Beeeeep! Beeeeep! Beeeeep!

    Driving around in this town can be stressful and a real nightmare sometimes. I always feel sorry for the tourists who come here and try to figure out where they are going. The roads can be poorly marked and one-way streets can be changed to the opposite direction with little or no notice.

    One could be driving into town and end up in massive congestion when, out of the blue, the sound of Beeeep! Beeeep! Beeeep! is heard. With that sound, all of the break lights in front of you come on. You know, for certain, that every other driver is thinking exactly the some thing you are: Where's the truck? What direction is it coming from? I hope it doesn't back over me!

I got a 'hint' of the life to come from a delivery truck, in reverse. The attention-getting, beeping sound made my ears perk up and I looked all around to be sure I was not in a position to be hit.

In the life to come, God will show us how He used the 'beeping' sound of our conscience to pull us up short, make us pause and focus our attention so that our actions would not cause harm to ourselves or others.

Sometime this week, think about how your conscience has forced you to take note of what you were doing. Whether you paid attention or not could have had serious repercussions for you, a loved one or a total stranger. God is giving you a 'hint' of what He has in mind for you and just how much He

~ HINTS ~

longs to protect you, sometimes even from yourself.

In the life to come, you will be shown how many emotional fender benders were avoided because you heard God's "Beeeeep! Beeeeep! Beeeeep!" deep down inside and paid attention.

~ 19 ~

"Prayer is not eloquence,
but earnestness."

Hannah More (1745-1833)

Who?

There are some people we meet in our lives who really get on our last nerve! Whether it is personality, attitude, demeanor or something you just can not put your finger on, you simply do not care for them. If you feel some individuals have actually hurt you or belittled you or been just plain mean, you bristle at the mere thought of having to be in the same room with them.

I got a 'hint' from God concerning those people I did not want to be around, particularly the ones I felt had hurt me. I prayed for them none-the-less. Now, do not be misled; my prayer would be for the well-being of certain individuals but I would never call their names. My prayer would go something like this: "Dear

God, please bless those for whom I have no desire, what-so-ever, to pray and You know exactly who they are!"

In the life to come, God will introduce me to all the people who prayed for me when they had no desire, what-so-ever, to do so. With an introduction from God, we will all be friends and all irritations, misunderstandings and insensitivities will completely evaporate. We will love our neighbor as we love ourselves because that is an actual element of the life to come.

Sometime this week, pray for that someone who knows just how to 'push your buttons' and really makes you 'crazy.' When you pray for someone like that, know that God is giving you a 'hint.' Someone else may well be praying for you in the same way. Neither of you have to mention names if it is

~ Hints ~

just too painful because God knows exactly who they are.

In the life to come, your prayers will gain you many, many eternal friends; far more than you have here on earth. God is just Great at multiplication.

~ 20 ~

"The exhibition of real strength
is never grotesque."

Robert Aris Willmott (d. 1863)

Surprise

I really like stone houses. They always seem strong and secure. Perhaps that idea stuck in my mind from my earliest days, having heard the story of the "Three Little Pigs." I do not know for sure; I just know that I like stone houses.

When I drive to and from work, my trip takes me down many of the lovely tree-lined roads around town. Many of the homes along the way are the ones I like. They are rather large and dissimilar, one from the other. I enjoy studying them, as time allows.

During the day, these houses really do not have a great deal to recommend them. They appear 'boxy' but sturdy, none-the-less;

'dependability' seems like an appropriate word for them.

When I go to work in the mornings, the sun has not come up. As I drive by those old homes, I notice that some of the owners have external lighting bathing their structures. Amazing things happen when light floods a subject. Those houses are lovely. All the textures of the stones show up and light ripples off the surfaces, showing all kinds of dimension. The cornices and gables stand out from the roofline, as proud as can be.

I have gotten a 'hint' of the life to come from old, stone houses. There are many people like those dependable, sturdy, weathered structures. In their day to day labors, their outward appearance, their quiet, unassuming manner, they draw little or no attention to themselves. These people go through life simply doing what ought to be done, without pomp and circumstance.

~ HINTS ~

Sometime this week, look around and observe someone you think is quite ordinary, nothing special, really, 'nothing to write home about.' Now, try and imagine that person in the most favorable light possible. God is giving you a 'hint' because, in the life to come, this is how God will reveal everyone's true dimensions. Illuminated by His light, all the depth, detail and character of each and every individual will shine forth for all eternity.

~ 21 ~

"We need to suffer
that we may learn to pity."

L. E. Landon (1802-1838)

Learning Curves

    Young and old alike have always been inspired by great athletes (not the ones who cheat); those who take the time and exert the effort to excel at some physical pursuit. The work done by true champions is edifying to all those who applaud their accomplishments. Strong individuals make us all want to be stronger; great competitors make all of us want to compete at higher levels. Those who 'shine' in their profession make us want to 'shine' in ours.

    What about those qualities that are not as obvious as athletic achievement?

    I have always wondered why some people have to suffer so much in their lives. What good comes from such pain? The more I think about it, the more I recognize what I have received from these mighty warriors. The individuals I know who have really had to do without in their lives have an affinity for their fellows who are without. The people who have experienced physical pain more easily identify with anyone in pain. Those who are emotionally pushed to the limit have a remarkable understanding of others undergoing emotional stresses. It would appear that those who suffer have exercised their emotional muscles and the world is the recipient of gifts such as empathy, pity, understanding, true charity and the ability to really listen.

God has given me a 'hint' of what awaits all of us. Just as great physical achievements are acknowledged in the here and now; in the life to come, those who identify with fellow tortured souls will hold a special place indeed. These will be God's champions because they revealed to us, while on earth, aspects of God's own personality. Understanding, wisdom, sympathy and all the intangible qualities that matter to us are fully contained in our God. Those who suffer are our constant 'hints.' The suffering endured in this life is the soil that allows all the most important parts of character to grow and bloom.

Who do you know who hears what you have to say better than anyone else? Who is your shoulder to cry on? Who tears up when you are in pain? The people you think of identify because they have been there.

Sometime this week, think about the special people in your life who seem the most perceptive about your moods and show the greatest understanding about what you are going through in your life. God is giving you a 'hint' of the life to come through those individuals. They are reflecting His great love, concern, pity and understanding of all that you have to endure. In the life to come, all of the gifts that came to you through your pain will be clearly revealed.

~ 22 ~

"Variety of mere nothings
gives more pleasure
than uniformity of something."

Jean Paul Richter (1765-1826)

Produce Department

    I truly enjoy walking through the produce department at the grocery store. Sometimes, I just stand there and wonder what an immigrant from a foreign country would think about so much abundance. In addition, I take in all the colors, shapes and textures around me. It is amazing. Redskin potatoes, yellow crookneck squash, green zucchini, celery stalks, crisp red, yellow and variegated apples, a lovely floral cauliflower, bumpy, rich green avocado, all on display. The simplicity and beauty of the display is everywhere to be seen. Why is there such a presentation in the super market? Well, each and every item is meant to end up revealing its inner self and nourishing humanity. What a great vocation.

God continually gives me 'hints' of the life to come at the grocery.

Why is anyone prejudice toward anyone else? God has placed the fat and the thin, the brown, black, white, yellow and, yes, variegated, all around us. He has placed the addict, the smoker, the tippler, the straight and the gay, the young and the old, the beautiful and the unattractive, on display all over the world. Why has He done this? If I can think of everyone I meet, all of whom share our common humanity, like I do the abundance before me in the produce section then maybe, some individuals will open themselves to me and nourish my mind, heart and soul. I know that this cannot happen if I only feed on the same kind of food day after day and year after year. God presents His great gifts to us in variety. I want to take full advantage of His gifts and appreciate each and every one of them throughout all eternity.

~ Hints ~

Have you ever taken time to notice variety all around you? Have you even gazed at a rainbow, the magnificence of fall leaves, the tall pines and the tiny clover? God is giving you 'hints' of the life to come every time you appreciate the importance of difference.

Sometime this week, try and say a sincere "Hello" to someone who seems different and whom you may have overlooked before. Do it often and perhaps the 'other' will open up and nourish you in a way you least expect. You can find wisdom, humor, life lessons, support and common ground all around you. Keep looking and you will have started to enjoy the life to come in the here and now.

~ 23 ~

"Light is the task
where many share the toil."

Homer (10th Century B.C.)

Canes, Walkers and Wheelchairs

    I work at a hospital. Day after day, I watch the Physical Therapists and the Respiratory Therapists walk patients up and down the halls. Everyone's efforts are directed at building up the ill person's stamina and helping them get strong enough to go home.

    God gives me 'hints' of the life to come each and everyday I go to work.

    When I pulled into the parking lot the other day I noticed an empty, red wheelchair, rolled up against a post. That caused me to think about all those tools that are put to use in aid and support of the weak.

I have thought about the times I suffered disappointments in my life and came through alright. How did I get OK? God was the 'cane' that supported me.

I have thought about the days following the loss of a career, not just a job, which I loved so much. I really doubted that I would ever feel good again; it was literally hard to breathe. God was the 'wheelchair' that moved me through the emotional devastation, to a better place.

When I lost loved ones, suddenly and tragically, God was the 'gurney' that transported my prostrate soul to the desire to go on living.

In the life to come, I will fully realize how many spiritual tools and pieces of equipment God used, throughout my life, to bring me safely to His dwelling place. I know that I will be thoroughly amazed at how often I was held up, strengthened, supported and consoled by a loving God; the Greatest Emotional Therapist ever.

~ Hints ~

Have you ever wondered just how you have had the strength to overcome your day to day stresses; your overwhelming losses; your "Why" questions?

This week, think about the 'hints' God continually gives you of the life to come by holding you up; sending you the perfect friend, just when you need one; instigating the phone call from someone far away who just wants to hear how you are doing. In innumerable ways, God has supported you through thick and thin and, in the life to come, you can tell God how much you appreciate all the tools He used to support you in your weakness.

~ 24 ~

"Give what you have.
To someone it may be better
than you dare to think."

Henry Wadsworth Longfellow (1807-1882)

Thank You!

From the time I was a little girl, I really loved to hear a certain singer. My Mama said that I would stop whatever I was doing and just listen. Once, she took me to a music store and the first album she bought for me was by that artist. There was something about that voice that made me feel good, deep down inside. Music can do that, you know.

As an adult, I was able to meet this marvelous person who had always held such a treasured place in my heart. Getting to know him, over a number of years, only deepened my respect and admiration for him. Here was someone who always used his God given gifts to the maximum. Knowing him was a great privilege.

God gave me a 'hint' of the life to come through a performing artist. I can see that God creates singers, dancers, film makers, artists of every kind, to inspire, soothe, give joy, incite sweet memories and lift us up. All creative people reflect their Creator; what a foreshadowing of the life to come.

When we arrive at our new life, we will be able to "Thank" every artist we have ever appreciated for the contributions they made to our earthly lives.

The dear performer I cared about so deeply has gone on to his reward but I look forward to the time when we will see one another again and hug, just the way we always did here on earth.

Sometime this week, think about musicians, singers or any performing artist who makes you happy. Do you sing along? Do you picture a loved one? Do you recall a

~ HINTS ~

special occasion in your life? If you do, God is giving you a 'hint'. In the life to come, you will be able to see, hear and re-experience all of the good things that creative people brought to your earthly life and thank them and their Creator.

~ 25 ~

"It is not enough to help the feeble up,
but to support him after."

William Shakespeare (1564-1616)

Healing Hands

    I am a great admirer of my sister. I really look up to her more than anyone else I know. She is quite extraordinary.

    When my brother, sister and I were growing up, my sister was tall and gangly and that made her self-conscious. Through all the uncomfortable years, her loving, generous heart always came shining through.

    While in high school, my sister volunteered at our local hospital. Caring for others seemed to be her real passion.

    Having married, had her children and seen them reach their teen years, she went to nursing school and achieved her heart's desire, being a registered nurse. Over the last thirty years, she has taken care of 'her'

Oncology patients with all the love and affection she gives to our entire family, each and every day.

God has given me a 'hint' through my sister's example. Her care giving, loving touch, concern for all who suffer, are a reflection of God's Own approach to us. In the life to come, we will realize how intimately God has been involved in our lives. It will become absolutely clear that God has always been our ultimate Care Giver. A 'hint' of this truth is beautifully represented by my sister's own life. Her response to the desire God placed in her heart, to care for others, has given me a greater appreciation for God's care for us all.

Sometime this week, think about someone you have seen open a door for someone else; pick up a child who has skinned a knee; taken the arm of an elderly person to give support

~ Hints ~

or simply smiled at a disabled stranger. God is giving you a 'hint' of the life to come when you appreciate these signs of caregiving. We all need to be picked up when we fall; smiled at when we are wounded; and given support each and every day. God is the very best nurse humanity has and we will fully realize that in the life to come.

~ 26 ~

"Our prayers should be for blessings in general, for God knows what is good for us."

Socrates (469-399 B.C.)

Dreams and Reality

At one time, I worked at the most wonderful place one could imagine. I looked forward to going to work each and every day. (As a matter of fact, one year, I worked 365 days. It was Great!) I would have done what I was doing for free, if that had been practical.

After twenty-five years of fun, absolute enjoyment, marvelous camaraderie, great professionalism, my 'home-away-from-home' drastically changed. Reason: New Management. After so many years, I was truly amazed at just what 'new managers' can do. The ability of some individuals, 'In Charge', to literally suck all of the joy out of a work environment can be shocking and very unnerving. All of the sudden, everything had to be scheduled, listed, nit-picked; all spontaneity ceased.

For close to five years, I told myself that things would surely get better. They didn't. At the same time, I had great losses in my family. So, my home life was drastically altered and my 'home-away-from-home' underwent the same kind of change. I felt adrift because I was. I know that I was just suffering too much to be a docile employee.

When I was told: "Your services are no longer necessary," I thought I would die. That is really the way I felt. Seemingly, God had not heard my prayers for everything to be alright and for those in control to understand what I was going through. Why should they? What did my feelings have to do with 'business?' Actually, nothing.

What was I to do? I did not know how to do anything else, after twenty-nine years, three months.

My sister recommended that I apply for a job at the hospital where she worked. She was well aware that I knew nothing about patient care but thought that my computer skills could be useful. She was right and I got a job, after training, taking off the physicians orders, first on a Cardiac unit and then, on the Oncology and Respiratory units.

~ HINTS ~

Several years later, the economy took a drastic down turn. One of the stable areas in the economy was in health care. Imagine that!

I truly got a 'hint' of the life to come from my unanswered prayer. God saw the whole picture and was taking care of me even when I didn't see it.

Sometime this week, try and recall some situation you prayed would change for the better but it didn't. Then, really ponder what God gave you that turned out to be better. You were given a 'hint.' God is always concerned about every aspect of your life and what is best for you. Sometimes, He says "No" to your prayer but only because of His love for you. In the life to come, all your "Why?" questions will be answered and you will understand just how much your life was nestled in loving hands.

~ 27 ~

"Evil is wrought by want of thought,
as well as by want of heart."

Edwin Paxton Hood (1820-1885)

Why Evil?

I have always wondered why evil seems to grow, like weeds, in our life experience. What possible 'hint' can I find from my encounters with hateful, insensitive or down-right evil individuals?

Maybe the answer lies in comparison. What would valor mean if there was no occasion to practice it? What good would empathy do if someone were not in pain? Why would we join together, to look out for one another, if there were no threats to safety and security and peace of mind?

God gave me a 'hint' of the life to come from thinking about all the horrible things that can occur in this life. The life to come will encompass all the 'cream' that has come to the top of our existence. Those who have borne great sorrow will experience the greatest joy; those who fought evil will have an eternal respite from battle; those who suffer at the hands of others will be lovingly soothed and experience everlasting comfort.

Comparison... How would I ever have anyone to admire and look up to if there were not an experience that made that person admirable or worthy of respect? I would never see any outstanding qualities of character if there had not been a challenge. Those who choose evil stimulate good in others; those who do harm promote healing from others; those who hate incite us to love. Comparison.

In the life to come, all the good that has arisen from evil will be rewarded and honored. Humankind will realize what full compensation means for all those who have 'fought the good fight.'

~ Hints ~

Who is it that you admire? Why? What evil or difficulty are they battling or have they overcome?

Sometime this week, think about someone you know who has stood for what is right and has met evil with good. Perhaps you can think of a person who spoke up when another was being ridiculed. Maybe you are that person. If so, acknowledge that fact in your heart and realize that God is giving you 'hints' of the life to come through your own experience, battles and good character.

~ 28 ~

"He picked something valuable out of everything he read."

Pliny, the Elder (23-79)

Once Upon A Time...

There are certain types of books I prefer to read over others. I like historical fiction but they are not my exclusive choice. If I happen to hear an interesting interview with an author, I may go get the book. If I am just browsing through the bookstore, I may select something that catches my eye.

I have read and re-read *A Christmas Carol* even when it is not the holiday season. *The Velveteen Rabbit* seems timeless to me. *The Bible, My Utmost for His Highest, The Immigrants, The Grass Crown, Big Russ and Me* have all held my interest and stirred my imagination. Some stories are so sweet that they have brought me to tears.

I have learned so much about the life to come from reading. That God created individuals, throughout history, who excelled at the written word, gives real insight into His interest in each and every person, since the beginning of time. While some may have used their writing skills to spread hate and misinformation and lead readers to a belief that their Creator is an ogre, only points to the perversion of a good gift. There are so many more that have used their gifts to edify, lift up and sometimes, just present a simple truth.

The written word is just one way our God has chosen to give us 'hints.' The inspiration which drives some individuals to take up the pen (or the keyboard) can open our minds to new ideas or tickle our funny-bones or offer us models of purposeful living. Writers may also teach us what we need to know or point out what evil, hate and error look like.

In the life to come, we will be able to honor all those who inspired us so much through their writing. We will have a complete understanding of how the written word lead us to God.

~ Hints ~

Sometime this week, think about something you have read or are reading. Does that work make you happy, lift your spirit or teach you some truth? Or, have you opened your mind and heart to a destructive message? If the latter is the case, stop right now! Your inner self is too precious to sully in any way, particularly by your reading habits.

In the life to come, God will show you all the 'hints' He has given you about His desire for your good. You will realize that all of the marvelous things you read were solid food for your spirit and the trashy, destructive and hateful were like poison.

~ 29 ~

"Light is the symbol of truth."

James Russell Lowell (1819-1891)

It's A Wrap

At one time, I did lighting for television and stage productions. My job, as I saw it, was to simply create a lovely and appropriate environment for an artist to perform within. I loved my job!

When I lit a musical piece or an interview, the whole point was to take the music, lyrics or the interview format under consideration and choose whatever furthered those aspects of the production. I always wanted the performer to look as fabulous as possible. The artist was the entire reason for my having a job to love.

There is a different approach to lighting that most people are more familiar with these days. It is lighting for lighting's sake. Some call it 'flash and trash.' In this case, lighting becomes an 'artist' too, as opposed to the actual performer. I am not a fan of that concept but I understand it. Everyone wants to get their money's worth and lighting is expensive.

God taught me so much about the life to come through my work and the way I perceived the job. I learned that He wants me to be as marvelous as I can possibly be. He wants me to be His STAR and He takes great pains to help me be my very best. Sometimes, I have had fits and starts in my life and I fight the pain that can come with progress but, that does not hinder God's work on my behalf.

In the life to come, I will look back and see every perfect scene God formulated to help me mature and grow. God was involved in my reaching my full potential and helped me become everything I was created to be. He was with me all the time. He was not into any 'flash and trash' effects but rather, He sought to show me the way home through gentle persuasion.

~ HINTS ~

Think about some difficulty in your life that, in retrospect, made you stronger. It wasn't until you had come through the situation and could look back that you saw what gains you had made, as a parent, as a teacher, as an employee or as a friend. Through all these experiences, God has given you 'hints' of the life to come. He set up the perfect environment for your growth. God's involvement in your life is not random, it is very personal. In all your struggles, hold on to the truth that you are loved and your will is respected and no circumstance will ever change that.

~ 30 ~

"Every man is a hero and an oracle to somebody, and to that person, whatever he says, has enhanced value."

Ralph Waldo Emerson (1803-1882)

To Teach

When I was in college, I was fortunate enough to be taught by an outstanding professor; some instructors are good but few are truly superior. I had such a truly superior teacher. The old saying: "Those who can, do and those who can't, teach," was shown for the gigantic lie that it is. I learned that first hand from the fine educator I had as a teacher.

My teacher placed a priority on putting what we were learning in text books into practice. As a matter of fact, the practice of what we were learning held more weight toward our final grade than rote knowledge from a text book.

This excellent instructor was always a source of encouragement and positive thinking. He always assumed that we were going to be able to accomplish all of our dreams once we left the college environs. I am certain that I was able to work in a profession I loved, for almost thirty years, due in large part to this outstanding teacher.

I got a 'hint' of the life to come from a dedicated, gifted professor. The phrase, "faith without works is dead" really meant something in the light of this teacher's emphasis. For him, book-knowledge without practical application was not learning.

All of the persons God has placed in my life to push and challenge me to 'do better,' 'be better,' and 'think deeper' have been 'hints' of God's interest in my complete fulfillment in the life to come

~ HINTS ~

Sometime this week, think about someone who has taught you a truth, taught you a skill, taught you a prayer or taught you what really matters. God is giving you a 'hint' of the life to come through the actions of anyone who has taught you anything at all. The accumulation of all the things you have learned has helped you to grow as a thoughtful, considerate, caring human being. The 'whole' person you are becoming will reach completion in the life to come.

~ 31 ~

"Man has sight; women insight."

Victor Hugo (1802-1885)

Lace

I do believe my sister-in-law can do everything well. She is a remarkable woman. One of her talents, always producing something lovely, comes from her gifted hands, plying a crochet hook. With a large hook, she produces the softest, warmest hats and scarves. On a cold and blustery day, nothing hugs you like her crocheted accessories. Those same fingers, using the smallest hook, creates lovely, patterned lace.

I have always gotten a 'hint' of the life to come from the large and the small. My sister-in-law brings this to mind as does my Creator. God gives me a 'hint' when I see hummingbirds. I stand at my kitchen window and watch those little creatures with absolute fascination. They hover beside the feeder and drink as much nectar as they can hold. I think God must have thought: I'll create the most amazing little birds I can think of and, when people see them, they will just love watching them.

In like manner, God placed fabulous orbs in the heavens for all to see. I stand in my driveway in the evening and look up. Seeing the crescent moon, with Mars, shining like a headlight, nestled up next to that moon, is truly awe inspiring. As my eyes get adjusted to the night sky, I begin to see twinkling stars scattered all over the heavens.

Yes, God gives me 'hints' of the life to come through the handiwork of my sister-in-law and His's own creation. In the life to come, every detail, large and small, will have been considered by our God and I will have a perfect place in the scheme of it all. I will feel unending pleasure in the small details and awe-struck by the bigger picture.

~ Hints ~

Sometime this week, think about someone you know who does small, detailed things well. Then, think about someone else who handles large projects with great proficiency. In your observations, God is giving you 'hints' of the life to come. He is the Master of all things, great and small and, in the life to come, you will know that reality.

~ 32 ~

"Call not that man wretched, who,
whatever ills he suffers,
has a child to love."

Robert Southey (1774-1813)

Little Ones

My Mama loved babies. When she was a child, her Mother would sometimes give her and her sister dolls for Christmas. My Mama told me that the day after Christmas, her sister would have two dolls. Mama would say: "They aren't real." She wanted to have her own, real babies to take care of and she certainly did do just that as she cared for my brother, sister and me.

I cannot recall, whether at the grocery, in an airport or in a foreign country, that a baby, upon making eye contact with my Mama, failed to raise it's little arms up to be held. Mama would always say: "Babies know when they are loved."

God gave me a 'hint' of the life to come every time I saw my Mama's encounters with babies.

We are all babies. In comparison to an Eternal God, no matter how long we live, we will always be babies in that relationship. When the time comes for us to make eye contact with our everlasting Father, each of us will raise our arms up to be held. At that time, we will know, just like my Mama said, that we are loved and always have been. Many times, the stresses of life hide this realization from us.

Sometime this week, think about the innocence of children and the look in their eyes when they are with someone they trust. When you see that look or that special smile or those little arms, reaching up, know that God is giving you a 'hint' of the life to come. He wants you to realize that you are acting

~ Hints ~

the way He will, by picking that child up and holding him close, rocking, smiling and laughing together.

Sometime this week, think about the fact that in the life to come, you are the child and you are loved.

~ 33 ~

"A miracle is a work exceeding the power of any created agent…"

Robert South (1634-1716)

Our Big Brother

My brother was very, very ill when he was five years old. He had meningitis and everyone thought that he would die. It was during the Second World War that he got so sick. So much of the medicine was going to the military but, my brother's Doctor managed to obtain the medicine he needed from a military base not far from our home. Even with that, my brother was not getting any better. The Doctor said that he needed an oxygen tent. Back then, there just was not an oxygen tent to be had.

In the room across from my brother's, was a wealthy, very sick, old man. He had the only oxygen tent. He overheard the nurses talking about the little boy across the hall. He called in his nurse and started taking off the oxygen tent from over his head. The nurse tried to stop him but to no avail. The man told her that he was an old man and had lived a full life and he wanted the little boy to have his tent. He said that the child should have a chance at a life now. With that, my brother got the oxygen tent.

Sometime later, my brother came out of his coma and regained enough strength to go home. The old man across the hall got to go home too. They both survived.

God gave our whole family a 'hint' of the life to come from the actions of the old man, across the hall. (I had not even been born yet,)

Our God is like that old man. He knows us but He also hears everything that is said about us and, in our own hearts, what we say about ourselves. He is like that old man, in that He wants to give us exactly what we need; not always what we want but always what we need.

In the life to come, we will know in just how many amazing ways God provided what we needed in this life and we never even realized it.

~ Hints ~

You may have some recollection of a need you had that was fulfilled in a most unexpected way. Perhaps you thought your need was met by sheer happenstance.

Sometime this week, think about some of your needs, not wants, and just how they were fulfilled. If you can recall just one (although I am sure there are many more), you will have gotten a 'hint' of the life to come. God is always aware of all your needs and longs to answer them, but only when the answer is in your best interest. The life to come will reveal to you that forever and always, God is on your side.

~ 34 ~

"To God, thy country and thy friend be true…"

Henry Vaughn (1622-1695)

Fidelity

I am not a cat person; I really like dogs. Our family always had a dog when we were growing up; the "Heinz 57" breeds, as my Daddy called them. As a child, I loved my dog. The one we had during my formative years followed my brother, sister and me everywhere we went. I think I realized then that whether I was happy, sad, good or bad, liked or disliked, my dog was just 'crazy' about me. He made no judgments as to my character, he just liked being by my side. Isn't that a marvelous realization?

In my adult life, at a time that found me in great distress, I had two friends who called me every week to see how I was doing. I had believed, falsely as it turned out, that I had a multitude of friends who cared about me. Wow, what a learning experience I had during such a difficult time. The gulf between friend and acquaintance is quite dramatic. Regardless of the number of years, true friends are few, while acquaintances may be everywhere.

God showed me 'hints' of the life to come from my own encounters with fidelity. Who can you trust? Who can you count on when things really get rough? A faithful hound was my first clue and two dear, true friends really brought the meaning of fidelity into clear focus for me. My friends were totally disinterested in what may have been said about me or what others may have thought about me, they simply cared about me. That was another very meaningful realization on my part.

In the life to come, I will see all of the ways God has been completely faithful to me, even when I have acted like His acquaintance instead of His friend. He is always faithful because that is His nature. I, on the other hand, continue to be a work in progress.

~ HINTS ~

Do you have one real friend (or maybe two, like me)? That friend is your 'hint' from God about your life to come. God wants you to know that should you say you do not even have one friend, you will always, yes, always have one in Him. True friendship and fidelity coexist. God is ever faithful and the true friend of all that He has created. He cannot deny His devotion to you because He cannot deny Himself. He will always be your friend, even if you continue to only be His acquaintance.

~ 35 ~

"The fountain of beauty is the heart…"

Francis Quarles (1592-1644)

WOW!

I have often wondered about 'beautiful' people...

I am not particularly attractive so, when I see someone who is obviously a beauty, I wonder how they feel about the person they see in the mirror.

In my working life, I was very fortunate, for many years, to work with some of the loveliest looking people in this town. The way they walked, wore their clothes, fixed their hair, put on their make-up and sometimes, when they just walked into a room, everyone would say: "WOW"! If the WOW was not actually spoken, it was what everyone was feeling inside.

Once, at a mall, I noticed a young man, working behind a kiosk, who was startlingly handsome. I walked over and told him so too.

I have gotten many 'hints' of the life to come from being around some beautiful people. My experience has taught me that some people are beautiful on the outside but not so much so on the inside. Sometime that revelation came from their words or actions. Others do compliment their outer beauty by their inner loveliness. Their demeanor displays how attractive they are in every way.

In the life to come, what each and every individual is, on the inside, will be seen by everybody else. In their new life, the now gorgeous, who were such wallflowers on earth, will be revealed for the generous, giving, understanding people they truly were in their earthly life. For those who did see their outer beauty only as the reflection of a gentle heart and a loving manner, they will surely have their reward. The revelation of true beauty in the life to come will surely elicit a "WOW" from everyone.

~ Hints ~

Do you know someone who is considered 'plain' or down right unattractive? Perhaps you see yourself that way. Sometime this week, just consider beauty when you see it. God will give you 'hints' of your life to come. Everyone's heart, way of thinking, intention... in other words, the real person, will come to light. I'll bet that in your life to come, you will be absolutely astonished by just who it is you see in the celestial mirror.

~ 36 ~

"Eyes will not see when the heart wishes them to be blind."

Lucius Annaeus Seneca (4 B.C.-65 A.D.)

Eyeglasses

When I was young I had to get eyeglasses. I cannot believe some of the frames I chose for them back then. I laugh out loud when I see some of the old photos we have around here. I really looked like a 'geek.' Some of the pictures are really funny. Between the school uniforms we had to wear, that made us look like we just came from a penal colony, and my glasses, one has to roll with laughter. Such 'loveliness' has been preserved for all time; unbelievable.

    I know that children get teased about having to wear glasses. My brother got picked on when he was young but, he turned out just fine. He was not about to let glasses or teasing prevent him from living a full life and accomplishing all of the goals he had set for himself. Nothing stood in the way of his enjoying life to the maximum.

I remember when I got my glasses. For me, it was a good day (even with some awful frames). I saw things I had been missing. They were not just an aid to help me excel in my school work; no, there was a whole beautiful world out there that opened up to me because of my glasses.

God gave me 'hints' of the life to come from having to wear glasses. Eyeglasses were only one example of the many things I needed and would need to become everything I am meant to be. Glasses to see; warm, saltwater gargle for my sore throat; good, old chap stick for the lips; bandaids for my cuts; effective prescription medications; all of these are some of the 'little' things that keep me going. Little things matter.

God's abundance, exemplified by all the creative minds that think up remedies for our bumps and bruises, will be revealed in all its fullness in the life to come. I believe that God will give me a pair of celestial glasses (with wonderful frames, I might add) when I meet Him. When I put them on, I will see how my life contributed to God's whole plan. Really, I will be able to say: "Well, that's why that happened. That's why those people acted the way they did. Now, I see!"

Sometime this week, think about something that you really needed but that you considered a disadvantage to you, particularly in your formative years. Pick anything that applies to your life, like glasses applied to mine. Try and imagine who it was that thought up that 'something' which actually improved your life.

In the life to come, God will give you a pair of celestial glasses too. You will see how he inspired each and every idea with your personal need in mind. God's concern for you is just that personal; He has an everlasting interest in you.

~ 37 ~

"We should worship as though the Deity were present."

Confucius (550-476B.C.)

Pews

In our family, Mama and my brother, sister and I attended one church and our Daddy another. I believed that this made us a stronger, more understanding and extremely close family unit.

As I grew up, I was very aware that some members and teachers in our church, ever so subtly, showed preferential treatment to those children whose parents practiced the same faith. Likewise, my Daddy's family members and his church community considered us not quite acceptable. Strange as it may sound, all of the slights only bound us together even more tightly as a family. We were so fortunate to have been raised the way we were and the passage of time has caused me to treasure all my childhood memories even more.

I remember, on special occasions, Mama would get us all dressed up in our finest clothes and we would go to church with our Daddy. In like manner, Daddy would go with us. I realized at a very young age that the respect my Mama and Daddy showed toward one another helped us to mature with an easy acceptance of difference and free of prejudice. What a marvelous gift we were given by our good parents.

Once, when my Mama was having coffee with others, after a church service, someone asked her why Daddy was not in "the church?" Before my Mama could respond, the minister spoke up: "Oh, he's in the church; he's just in a different pew." I will never forget that statement. God gave me a huge 'hint' of the life to come through our minister's reply. I am certain that everyone will be truly overwhelmed when, in the life to come, they see just how many people, from 'different pews,' are rejoicing with their God.

~ Hints ~

Have you ever felt slighted or looked at with disdain because of a perceived difference? Have you ever looked at someone else in a preconceived way because of cultural, religious or ethnic differences? Sometime this week, think about it. In reactions to you or from you toward others, God is giving you 'hints' of the life to come. There are many, many 'pews' in this life and an infinitely understanding Creator will welcome whomever He pleases to His home. By exercising our limited judgment as to who might be acceptable, we make our God tiny, petty and unperceptive like us. We should try and think about His many 'pews' instead and how insightful our God is, for He always understands the heart.

~ 38 ~

"Work is as much a necessity to man as eating and sleeping."

Karl Wilhelm Humboldt (1767-1835)

The Best Pancakes in the World

When I was in elementary school and my sister was just starting high school, Mama took us to get registered for our classes. After that was done, she said that she was going to take us to a restaurant that had just opened. With that, we all went for pancakes.

Our waitress was an attractive, personable, red head and took our orders without a pad or pen. I was wide-eyed. She never wrote anything down and yet, our orders arrived just the way we had specified. Our waitress had filled every detail of our orders just right.

I have gone to that same restaurant for over forty years now and our precious waitress has always done her exceptional job, with a wonderful smile. We have never left the place without a hug. (Only in the last few years did she cut back on her hours and finally retire.)

From the first time I saw how our waitress did her work, I hoped to be as good at anything I tried to do as she. There have been few people I have respected and held in as high esteem as this fine lady. She did her job efficiently but with little or no fanfare.

God really gave me a 'hint' of the life to come from my long association with a dedicated lady, doing honorable work. She is truly a good example in my life.

I believe the life to come will be populated with many unheralded 'good examples.' God will honor these noble souls who may never have been called by their first names while on earth. God knows each and every one of them on a first name basis and there will be hugs-all-around for their good work.

~ Hints ~

Have you ever received good service or perhaps exceptional service from someone you never even looked in the eyes? Did you just take it for granted that you were only getting what you paid for? Perhaps, you overlooked your 'hint' of the life to come.

Sometime this week, pause when you are being assisted, in any way. Take a second; just look at the one who has put himself or herself at your service. If the job they do is not all that good, ask God to help them improve; if the service is really good, thank God for that person's fine effort. Also, take time to realize that both kinds of encounters may well have been with possible fellow inhabitants in your life to come.

~ 39 ~

"A wise man is never less alone
than when he is alone."

Jonathan Swift (1667-1774)

Electronics

Text massages, e-mail, twitter, and cell phones are all ordinary modes of communication these days. I am really amazed when I see young people texting, like crazy, regardless of where they are. It is so interesting. Once, at dinner, I observed my niece as she was eating. There she sat, fork in her right hand, cell phone in the left. She had a white-knuckle grip on that phone. I had to laugh and, when I called her attention to her behavior, she laughed too. She finds it extremely difficult to function without her phone. Something about that makes me feel sorry for her. Some behavior really exemplifies just how fearful people can be of isolation. Being by one's self does not have to equate to being alone.

    I have always had a preference for face-to-face, one-on-one communication. I need to see facial expression and body language so I can really tell how the conversation is going. For me, the phone is only for minimal information: "When and where do we meet?" The way I see true interaction is a 'hint' of the life to come. There is not a need for electronics when I am having a talk with God. I have always told others that communication with God is like express mail but there is no postage necessary. Isn't that great? Visiting with God here and now is perfect preparation for the life to come.

    Sometime this week, put all gimmicks and electronic forms of communication aside and try to express your feelings as simply as possible. You can do this with a loved one or a close friend or, your very best friend, God. You can share all of your most intimate feelings and your greatest difficulties with absolute candor. You never have to fear being misunderstood when you are talking, one-on-one, with God and that is your biggest 'hint' of the life to come. You can become so comfortable with this kind of communication that, in the life to come, you will not have to familiarize yourself with the process. Try it. Over time, this may well become your very favorite way of carrying on a conversation. It is definitely mine.

~ 40 ~

"We never seem to know what anything means till we have lost it."

Orville Dewey (1794-1882)

Gone But Never Forgotten

At one time in my life, I worked for a marvelous organization. Many of those with whom I worked were much older than I. Each and every one was a gifted, wonderful person. They had a wealth of life experience and being around such individuals was a great pleasure. This was a remarkable time of learning for me and also a time of hour upon hour of rib cracking laughter.

Since so many of my co-workers were up in years, I never knew, from week to week, just which individual might have passed on to the life to come. Having developed such love and devotion for all these fine folks and, recognizing the age discrepancies that existed between us, I made it a point of never failing to offer each and every one a good wish, a "hope you have a wonderful week," or a personal greeting of some kind, every time I saw them. You see, I did not know if I would see them again in this life. God gave me so many 'hints' of the life to come from this work experience. Each association brought me so much joy. I cannot possibly calculate all that I learned from being around so many precious people.

So many good friends are no longer with me but they are also never very far away. They are not forgotten. God has certainly not forgotten them either and all the love and friendship we shared here will continue, for all time, in the life to come.

Sometime this week, think about those you live with, work with or spend your free time with. Never pass up a chance to offer a kind word, a simple greeting, a thoughtful

~ HINTS ~

gesture or a good wish to them. You may not have the opportunity to do so tomorrow. That realization is a 'hint' about the life to come. Another 'hint' is a belief that love never ends and all those you have loved and cared about still love you too. Most importantly, they are dearly loved by their Creator and He will hold them close until you have the opportunity to say "Hello" again in the life to come.

~ 41 ~

"Too many cooks spoil the broth."

Balthazar Gerbier, Discourse of Building (1662)

Recipes

I don't cook all that much but I really enjoy a good meal.

Even though I do not spend a great deal of time in the kitchen, now and then I do like to prepare a dish or a dessert that I consider one of my favorites. I really find it fascinating to combine a bunch of ingredients and end up with something altogether different from any of the single items that went into it.

The terminology in cookbooks is very interesting. Words like 'cream,' 'beat,' 'sift,' 'fold,' 'cool,' 'heat,' 'turn out' really carry weight when one is creating something wonderful.

One of my favorite recipes is the one for an old-fashioned, sour cream pound cake. The end result of this baking extravaganza is awesome, though 'heavy'. It is incredibly tasty. It is even good for breakfast, with a steaming cup of coffee.

The process of creating something wonderful has really given me a 'hint' of the life to come. Creaming a great deal of butter and sugar together is not an easy task. (I have bruised the palm of my hand by doing it.) Beating eggs, one at a time, until a mixture is satiny smooth can be very important to a good outcome. Baking at 350 degrees can really heat things up.

In the life to come, I believe God will show me the care and time He took to measure, sift, combine and bake all the ingredients that made up my life. I will fully realize just how much He loved what He had made; how much He loves me.

~ Hints ~

If you enjoy cooking or only doing so because you must, pause the next time you start the process. Look at each of the items you choose. God is giving you 'hints.' With all the cooking you have to do, think about all of the time it took to get a meal on the table.

In the life to come, God will reveal to you one of His best and very favorite creations. You will see the time, effort, and the multitude of ingredients that went into it. It will be clear how tears, laughter, gain, loss, joy and sorrow were precisely combined in you and how God's perfect timing brought you Home.

~ 42 ~

"God is a circle
whose center is everywhere,
and circumference nowhere."

Empedocles (490-430 B.C.)

Motives

Years ago, when I was much younger, a friend of mind committed suicide. He was a talented young man and had the face of an angel. I guess he was in the kind of pain one doesn't share with loved ones or close friends or anyone. I never had a clue that he was hurting so badly.

This young man had a sweet girlfriend. She was devastated when he died. She called me and asked if I thought the love of her life went to hell? She had been taught that God "sent" people to hell who committed suicide. Well, once I got my breath back, I asked her a simple question: "Would you send him to hell?" "Of course not," she replied. "I loved him!" I asked her how she could presume that she loved him more than his Creator, Who knew him completely and understood everything about him and loved him totally? If she would not send him to hell how could she possibly worship a God she thought would do such a thing? Attributing horrible motives to God is one of the saddest things we humans do.

At another time in my life, I heard a group of people with whom I worked talking about the diseases and disasters God 'sends' to punish people because they are sinful and do not do what He wants them to do. That made me so angry and sad. I told them, flat out, that I refused to worship "their ogre, insensitive, uncaring and uninvolved-god." If their god held a ball bat and plagued his own creation, I felt sorry for them and they should reconsider their belief system.

I have received so many 'hints' about the life to come from these, as well as so many other experiences. The life to come will be a true reunion of all lovers with Love Itself. There are no dictators, no villains there. God loves everything that He has made. There are no hateful characteristics in His nature and we are incredibly misguided to attribute such motives to our God. The life to come will clearly show us how pitiful such beliefs were.

~ Hints ~

Try and always think well of God. If you find yourself attributing some evil or disaster or illness to Him, purge such ideas from your mind. Refuse to ever entertain such thoughts about your loving Creator and dismiss those who espouse such ideas.

Every time you care for someone, love someone, protect someone, God is giving you a 'hint' as to His nature. Your actions are only tinny-tiny 'hints' because God's goodness cannot be calculated by our childlike minds. Any good you can do is only a reflection of God, Who is Good itself; any love you feel is only a reflection of God, Who is Love itself; any 'truth' you think you know is only a reflection of God, Who is Truth itself. Sometime this week think about these things.

~ 43 ~

"Rescue me from my persecutors,
for they are too strong for me."

Psalm 142:7 NAB

Dresses

Did you know that brown cows give chocolate milk; white and brown cows give buttermilk; white cows give homogenized milk? Did you know that Black Angus cattle are really buffalo?

When we were little, my brother, sister and I used to spend time out on our Daddy's family farm. His Mother, sister and brother-in-law worked the farm. His father had died before I ever met him. Our aunt's husband, our dear uncle, told us all about cows and buffalo. (I can still hear my Daddy laughing when we explained it all to him.) But, if our uncle said something was so, it was so! This short, chunky, little farmer, in his overalls, was such a precious part of our young lives that we believed everything he said and writing about him now makes me happy.

How our uncle became part of our family is quite a story. He and his brother were living at an orphanage. One day they ran away and came charging up to the door of my Daddy's farm house. The runaways were just about the same age as my Daddy and his sister and two brothers. They were about six and eight years old. They had shown up wearing dresses because they thought it was the only way they could escape and it worked.

When the authorities caught up with the boys and wanted to return them to the orphanage, my Grandfather said: "Oh no, I'll keep 'em and raise 'em just like my own boys." So, a family of six turned into a family of eight.

I grew up with a 'hint' from my uncle's story and my grandfather's generosity. My uncle had come, running every step of the way, looking for safety and my grandfather said: "Come on in."

This is exactly what our Father does for us in the life to come. If we are running in His direction, He will swing the door open. It doesn't matter what we are wearing; the scars of life, the bloody noses of

~ Hints ~

disappointment, the bruises of fractured relationships and sleepless nights. If we are running in His direction, that is all we need to do. A "Welcome Home" awaits us.

Sometime this week, think about the direction in which you are running. Do not spend your time going the wrong way. You know the difference. If you have any questions about it, seek out good advice from someone trustworthy and a person you respect.

Right now, your life may be very difficult, for a myriad of reasons. Even your present difficulties can be 'hints' if you do not let them deter you from running in God's direction, for safety, wearing your 'emotional dresses' if necessary. Seeking God's help, now, is a great preparation for all that awaits you in the life to come.

~ 44 ~

"All that I am, or hope to be,
I owe to my angel mother."

Abraham Lincoln (1809-1865)

Anticipation

I work with the sweetest nurse. She is the Charge Nurse on our Oncology unit most weekends. At this time, she is expecting her fourth child; her fourth boy, as a matter of fact. Yesterday, she just happened to say, to no one in particular, that she could hardly wait "for this baby to get here. I think he really is going to be cute. Besides, I need some little toes to play with; toes that don't already have mud on them."

She and her husband have already picked out a name. When she told me the name she said it so sweetly that it almost brought tears to my eyes. Each day that we work together, I sidle up to her and ask her the baby's name, just so I can hear her say it in that very special way of hers.

God has given me a 'hint' of the life to come from working with this marvelous woman. Not having had any children of my own, the awe I feel about the coming motherhood of my friend inspires me.

I think that God is like my friend. He knows each and everyone of us by our name and when He says our name, the sound is so sweet that the celestial population gets all teary-eyed. That's how much God is interested in us, just the way my friend is interested in her baby, yet to come.

In the life to come, we will be present with God, like mother and child. He will be so glad to have us there to share His joy. The love and happiness we experience with Him will know no bounds.

~ HINTS ~

Sometime this week, think about a mother and child you know, maybe you and your own mother or you and your child. That closeness, that relationship, is God's 'hint' to you about your life to come with Him.

I understand that not everyone has had good relationships in their own families. But, even those who do not personally experience the love and devotion of parent and child have seen it in other's lives. Just recall where you have seen such unselfish love and realize that God is giving you a 'hint' of His total love and commitment to you.

~ 45 ~

"...the noise of thunder was only noise."

Anonymous

Be Still

We really live in a noisy world. There seems to be 'racket,' as my Mama called it, everywhere. Ministers that scream (my ears work just fine, thank you very much), earbuds 'in' all the time, souped-up cars and trucks, boom-boxes, arguments; 'racket', 'racket' everywhere!

I have always liked the story about the man who went up on a mountain, for safety, and hide in a cave. God told him to go to the mouth of the cave because the Lord would be passing by. The man experienced strong and heavy winds rending the mountains and crushing rocks. He saw earthquakes and fires. The Lord was not present in any of these things. Then, the man heard a tiny, whispering sound. The Lord was in that tiny sound.

I really get a 'hint' of the life to come from quiet moments. They can be hard to find in this hectic world but it is so important to try. When I can find time to be still, I really start to hear things, like birds, wind chimes, bumble bees but, best of all, tiny breezes playing in the trees. The tiny breezes make the tree limbs sing and bring the aroma of fresh flowers with it and even the church bells in the distance can be heard. I believe that the Lord is present in the respites we take from the noise.

In the life to come, the quiet moments will have great meaning. We will hear many of the sweet sounds we were unable to hear in this life due to all the 'racket.' We will understand that God was not in the 'racket.'

~ Hints ~

You really must try and find some quiet time for yourself. You do not have to 'do' anything; just be still. Sometime this week, make a real effort to step away from the break-neck speed of your life. There are so many 'hints' you can receive when you find a quiet place and just listen with your heart. Inspiration is available to you but it cannot get in for all the confusion around you. Happy memories can come and refresh you when they can find an opening. Dreams are all around but they cannot develop because it is just too noisy. Sometime this week, do something about this and begin to sense one aspect of the life to come.

~ 46 ~

"It is a little thing to speak a phrase of common comfort…"

Sir Thomas Taifourd (1795-1824)

Doughnuts

I do not believe that I used a pacifier when I was a baby. My Mama was not a big fan of 'foolers' but, it seems that most babies have them these days.

When I was little, I had the most wonderful stuffed animals; my preference was bears and it still is. As a matter of fact, when I was at work one day, one of the guys I was working with was musing about just what he should give his girlfriend for her birthday. I told him to go out and get the biggest stuffed animal he could find and give it to her. He thought that was a 'stupid' idea. That figures.

How about that <u>Peanuts</u> character with the blanket?

I have been 'down' or 'blue' from time to time and just petting my puppy, tweaking him behind the ear, has helped me to feel better. Talking to him helps me too, even if there are some who say that dogs do not understand it when you talk to them; my dog does indeed understand, so there.

When my nephew went to West Point, all the upperclassmen had their stuffed bears from their childhood right there with them. My nephew had my brother send his bear to him.

I bring doughnuts to work for the techs and nurses with whom I work (and for me too of course). Doughnuts have always been called 'comfort food' by everyone at work.

I have gotten many 'hints' of the life to come from all those things that give comfort. The one thing I have found that offers the greatest comfort is a hug from someone who really cares about me. In the life to come, everyone who has ever needed any kind of consolation will receive it when they get their hug from the God who loves us all.

~ Hints ~

Have you ever thought about why a pacifier calms a baby or a soft blanket lulls a child to sleep or a warm glass of milk helps you rest? These represent only a small portion of all the things that give you comfort in your life's journey and each and every one is a 'hint' for you. Try and think about that sometime this week.

In the life to come, God will show you how often He was right there with you as you held your stuffed toy or were embraced by an understanding friend. He was so glad you had the comfort you needed and He will reveal to you all the ways He eased your pain and you failed to recognize His loving hand at work.

~ 47 ~

"…to be simple is to be great."

Ralph Waldo Emerson (1803-1832)

An Apple and an Orange

 I do not believe I have ever known anyone that loved Christmas the way my Daddy did. I can truly say that was his season. Let me be clear, my Daddy was in no way involved with the commercial aspects of the holidays; not by a long shot.

 Ever since I was a child, I could remember the sound of a nutcracker at work. We had these wooden bowls that Mama kept full of whole pecans, English walnuts and Brazil nuts. She bought them by the bag during the holidays. My Daddy sat in his easy chair and would crack open a nut or two. I always came running at the sound. I would watch as his big hands, ever so gently, popped open the nutshell to reveal two perfect halves. He would hand one to me and he'd eat one. Oh, the Brazil nuts were a challenge to get out without crushing them but my Daddy could do it. I still have not mastered that trick.

Now, on to another seasonal treat... Daddy would take out a sleeve of buttery crackers, a stick of summer sausage and a block of cheese to create a marvelous, little, tasty snack. He always sliced everything with the pocket knife he carried with him all the time. As a child, I loved to watch his every move. He would slice each goody, put the whole thing together, with a nice blob of mustard, and hand me one. Yum-yum. The memory makes my mouth water to this very day.

It was always the little things that made the Christmas season so appealing to my Daddy. He was a simple, good man. Daddy would tell us about when he was young and how he and his siblings usually got an apple, an orange and a few pieces of hard candy in their Christmas sock. That was it.

I learned so much about the life to come from all the 'hints' my Daddy showed me through his enjoyment of the simple things. God wants us to see His hand in all the little things. He created the wonderful halves of

~ HINTS ~

the walnuts for my Daddy to share with me. Our pleasure in that moment will be eternally multiplied in the life to come.

Have you thought about a small, sweet memory lately? Perhaps you have one that makes your mouth water the way mine does when I see a stick of summer sausage. Sometime this week, think about your dearest, most treasured memories as 'hints' of the life to come. In every instance of joy you experience in this life, God is there too. Few, if any, of us will ever have a 'burning bush' experience but we do encounter our God in the little things. He is just that involved in our life and, in the life to come, we will see the 'whole' of all those tiny parts. Together, they will equal complete happiness; joy on top of joy; the apple, orange and hard candies of eternity.

~ 48 ~

"Jingle Bells, Jingle Bells,
Jingle All the Way."

James Lord Pierport (1822-1893)

Sleigh Ride

Many of the joys of my life revolved around the ability to do things to make my Mama happy. Only as an adult did I realize just how much my Mama sacrificed, did without, worked and prayed for me and every member of our family. She put off things she might have wanted so that we would not have to. Through it all, she had dreams too. She set her dreams and wishes aside so that our dreams could come true.

One of the things that my Mama dreamed of doing was riding through the snow in a horse-drawn sleigh. She loved snow. She talked about 'her sleigh ride' from time to time, especially when it would snow at our house, which it just didn't do all that often.

Needless to say, even when it did snow around here, there was rarely enough to make a snowman, much less ride through in a sleigh.

At one point, I was able to plan a little surprise for my Mama. I planned a trip for us to Lake Tahoe, in the winter. Tahoe is a marvelous place to be, particularly with the snow falling. We had a room, on one of the upper floors of our hotel, looking out on a forest of towering trees. The snow resting on the limbs was beautiful and my Mama would just sit at the window and take it all in. During our stay, we were able to take the dream sleigh ride. Next to our hotel, in an open field, the rides were offered. The excursion followed the old Pony Express trail. We were able to take a ride in a one-horse, open sleigh. Can you believe it? As we rode along, we looked down on that lovely blue jewel, Lake Tahoe. My Mama was thrilled, as was I.

God gave me a 'hint' of the life to come from the enjoyment I saw on my Mama's face during her sleigh ride.

God has planned all kinds of 'dreams-coming-true-moments' for us when we come

~ Hints ~

to stay at His house. He is excited, contemplating the looks on our faces when we experience everything He has prepared for us in the life to come.

Have you ever done something special for someone you care about? Have you planned just that right experience, at just the right time, and in just the right place? Well, sometime this week, think about the 'hint' God has given you about Himself, through your own actions. God has planned the perfect experience, at the perfect time, and in the perfect place for someone special, whom He loves... you. It will all happen for you in the life to come.

~ 49 ~

"To behold is not necessarily to observe..."

Karl Wilhelm Humboldt (1767-1835)

The Kitchen Window

When I get up in the morning, the first thing I do is head for the kitchen to make coffee. That first cup of coffee is so good and I really look forward to it.

As I am preparing the coffee, I feel there are eyes watching my every move. Sure enough, there are. As I peep out of my kitchen window, there he is...my puppy. We play this peep-pie game all the time and it always makes me laugh. My dog is very funny. When we play our game, he sits, looking in the window ('cause sometimes, I pretend not to see him), still as a statue, not moving a muscle. Then, I wave my hand and he comes, tearing a path to my back door. Just before he starts running, he licks his lips (he licks 'em every time). When he reaches the back door, there I am, holding a 'cookie' (it's really a dog biscuit). Now, he must sit to get the 'cookie' and he doesn't like to sit! We perform this charade all the time and I never fail to laugh.

I watch my dog off and on during the day. He is afraid of cats; I believe a cat must have slapped him on the nose because he has a scar there. He dozes in the sun, sometimes resting his head on a stepping stone with his body in the grass. I even caught him on day, up in a straight chair on the porch, his paws hanging over the seat, head nodding and jerking, nodding and jerking as he tried to nap. I took a picture. Yes, my dog is very funny.

I have gotten many 'hints' of the life to come from watching my puppy. I think God watches me with far greater enjoyment and concern than I have for my dog. I believe He smiles at me all the time and is sad when I get emotionally 'slapped'; He understands when I do not want to sit still in this life; He entices me to run to Him for encouragement, every chance I get. I think He is near me when I am at rest and I feel refreshed when I awake.

I believe God must have a very lovely kitchen window too.

Sometime this week, think about something or someone you observe that gives you joy; someone who simply makes you happy by your seeing them living their daily lives. You are receiving many, many 'hints' by all that you see. You yourself are exhibiting a tiny 'hint' of how much God enjoys your life, your joys; just your being makes Him happy.

In the life to come, you will truly understand just how directly involved God is and has always been in your life. You are His unique creation and your life matters to Him.

~ 50 ~

"The heart of the giver makes the gift dear and precious."

Martin Luther (1483-1546)

Old Broadway

For many years, I was in a position to plan trips and give gifts to my family and friends. As a matter of fact, my Mama, sister and I traveled all over the world together. We love to see new and exotic places and I was able to make that possible for us, often.

Unbeknownst to me, my sister had always wanted to do something unique and special for me. I had no idea.

Well, one day, while we were having lunch, I noticed that my sister seemed to be terribly excited about something. She was grinning from ear to ear. She was SO animated. Finally, she said that she could not hold it in any longer and she had to tell me something. I told her to go ahead; I just could not imagine what she was going to say.

She knew that I had admired a certain actor for many years. She had seen a television interview with that particular actor (I had not). In the interview, the performer mentioned that he was going to be doing a Broadway show. Well, on hearing that, my sister 'pulled out all the stops' and worked for quite some time to plan a trip to New York for us. Not only that, she had gotten tickets to that Broadway show; not just any tickets but front row, center. All of this is what she could hardly wait to tell me. Needless to say, the lunch I had ordered just sat on the table and got cold. I was as excited as my sister by this time and had absolutely no appetite at all.

What a wonderful 'hint' my dear sister gave me of the life to come. I believe that God has planned, from all eternity, to give us every good gift. When we reach our new life we will see that He has prepared a celebration for us, better than anything we ever could have dreamed of. That is how our Creator is. He is much more excited about His plans for us than my sister was that day at lunch.

~ Hints ~

Sometime this week, think about a time when someone planned a special surprise just for you. It was a 'hint'. God has always used wonderful occasions in your life to help you look toward your ultimate happiness with Him. You need 'hints'; we all do, Think about every special gift you ever received and realize what an insight God is giving you of the life to come.

~ 51 ~

"All of the rarest hues of human life take radiance and are rainbowed out in tears."

Gerald Massey (1828-1907)

Christmas Eve

As a child, I cried every Christmas Eve and simply could not go to sleep. I was just too excited! My Mama would sit beside my bed and pat me until I finally fell off to sleep.

Oh, the joy of Christmas morning. All the tears were forgotten as my brother, sister and I ran to the tree to see what Santa had left for us.

It was only when I grew up that I realized how hard my parents worked to make Christmas special for us. I had never thought how tired my Mama must have been, after patting me to sleep, for who-knows-how-long, and then fixing Christmas for all of us.

God gave me a 'hint' of the life to come and I see that clearly now as I look back on those Christmases, so many years ago.

Before we close our eyes on this life, I believe that God will be patting us to sleep. When we awake, we will see all that our God has planned for our eternal happiness. We will fully appreciate all that God has done in preparation for our awakening. We will come to life and say: "This is better than all my childhood Christmases combined!"

Have you ever been so excited about some upcoming event that you could not sleep? Has the anticipation of a special occasion brought tears to your eyes?

All of your occasional excitement and expectations are only 'hints' of what awaits you.

~ Hints ~

This week, think about a very special occasion you remember. Try and recall just how you felt and savor the feeling all over again. When you do that, you will come to know that it is only a 'hint' of the life to come.

~ 52 ~

"To be honest, as this world goes, is to be one man picked out of ten thousand."

William Shakespeare (1564-1616)

Hide and Seek

As I think about it, there are not many people who really know me for the person I truly am. They may know a little bit here and a little bit there but the person I really am is not so obvious. Why is that?

Over our lifetime, we have so many experiences, good and bad. I know I have. Each time an honest expression, on my part, elicited a negative reaction or a scowl from someone, I could sense myself withdraw a little. I would feel that I must not make that mistake again. Over time, being forthright can become difficult. I wonder if other people 'hide' too.

I have gotten so many 'hint' of the life to come from being an 'adult' in this world.

Being an 'adult' these days can equal 'hiding' most of the time. "Don't say that out loud!" "Just get along, will ya'?" "Being a 'yes man' secures your job." The lesson: If you 'hide', you survive.

One must certainly deal with the reality of the world in which we live. However, holding true feelings inside can eventually cause an explosion. I have found that there is a wonderful solution for this problem; I express all of my true feelings to the One Who knows the 'real' me.

In the life to come, God and I will certainly not be strangers. We will continue the honest relationship that was started in the here and now. I tell Him everything and He gives me endless 'hints' of His concern for me. With God, I can carry on no-holds-barred communication. It is a great privilege to be able to do that. There is no better Friend in my life and we grow closer with every passing day.

~ Hints ~

Do you 'hide'? Guess what? You never have to do that again. You do live in the real world but you have that special Person you can really open up to. Isn't that great?!

God is giving you a big 'hint' of your life to come. You see, you can tell His any and every thing. He loves you completely and understands your every struggle and frustration. You can yell, ask "Why?" share a great joy or an incredible disappointment. You have a never-failing Friend, God. The relationship you cultivate with your Best Friend will never have to end, ever. When you start to share everything with Him, He shares consolation, peace and understanding with you. That is what friends do for one another. Think about that this week and rejoice in the unending, honest relationship you have with your God.